SHAPE SAFARI

Written by Captain & Cat

Illustrated by Mike Goldstein

Let's go on a
SHAPE
SAFARI

WE'RE GOING ON A SHAPE SAFARI, AND LOOKING ALL AROUND!

WE'RE GOING ON A SHAPE SAFARI, AND WE'RE HEADED TO THE TOWN!

I SEE A HOUSE OVER THERE. AND YOU KNOW WHAT? IT'S ALSO A SQUARE! TRIANGLE ROOF AND RECTANGLE DOOR.

COME WITH US AND WE'LL FIND MORE, MORE, MORE!

Shape
Safari

WE'RE GOING ON A SHAPE SAFARI,
AND LOOKING UP AND DOWN.
WE'RE GOING ON A SHAPE SAFARI,
AND CRUISING THROUGH THE TOWN!

STOP
SCHOOL BUS

COME ALONG
AS WE RIDE THE BUS,
IT'S JUST A RECTANGLE
CARRYING US.

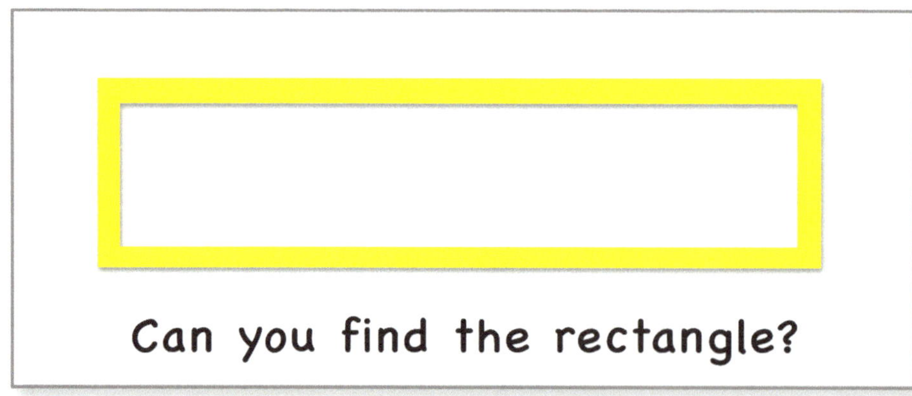

Can you find the rectangle?

STOP
SCHOOL BUS

UP AHEAD,
WE SEE A TRAFFIC LIGHT...
A BOX WITH THREE CIRCLES
SHINING BRIGHT.

YELLOW CIRCLE...
GO SLOW, SLOW, SLOW

RED CIRCLE...
STOP!

GREEN CIRCLE...
NOW WE GO! GO! GO!

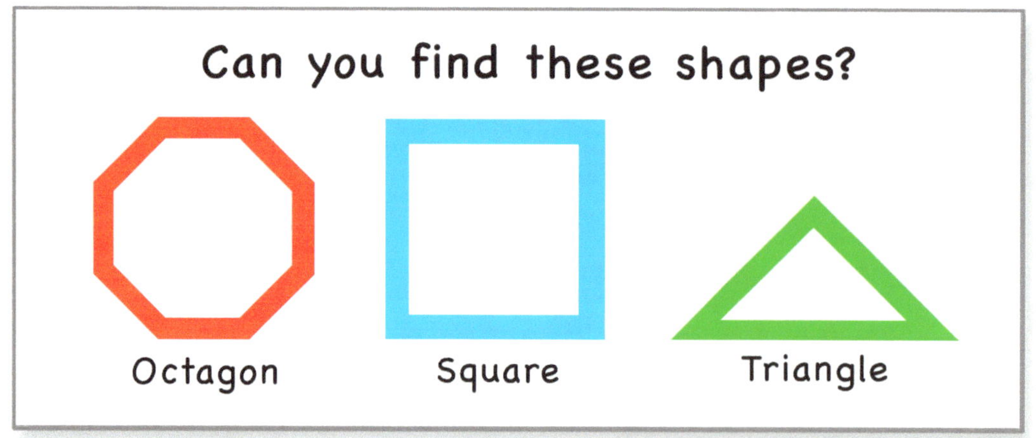

STOP
SCHOOL BU

WE'RE GOING ON A SHAPE SAFARI AND FINDING LOTS OF EACH. WE'RE GOING ON A SHAPE SAFARI AND HEADING TO THE BEACH!

ON THE SAND
AND WITHIN OUR SIGHTS,
RECTANGLE TOWELS
AND DIAMOND KITES.

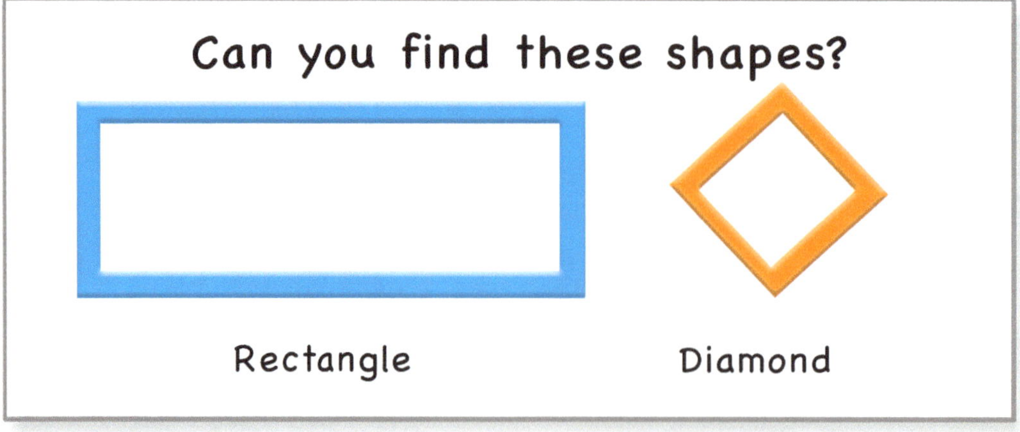

UNDERWATER ON THE CORAL REEF, A BABY SHARK WITH TRIANGLE TEETH!

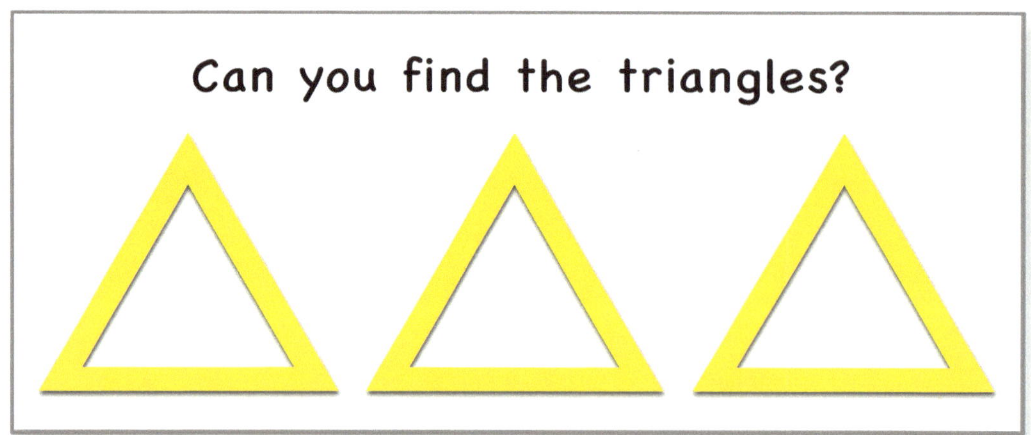

CIRCLE URCHINS WITH SPINY SPIKES. A HORSESHOE CRAB THAT DOES WHAT HE LIKES!

Can you find these shapes?

Circle

Horseshoe

DO-DO-DO-DO-DO
SHAPES

DO-DO-DO-DO-DO
SHAPES

DO-DO-DO-DO-DO
SHAPES

How many shapes
can you find?

AND THAT'S OUR SHAPE SAFARI, HOPE YOU ENJOYED THE RIDE. ON THE NEXT SHAPE SAFARI, DO YOU WANT TO BE THE GUIDE?

Hot
Cocoa
milk

Seek & Find

Hey friends, can you go back through Shape Safari and find these items? When you find the item place a ✓ on the blank provided. Good luck!

2 cannonballs.. ______
A broom.. ______
A singing fire hydrant .... ______
A cat.. ______
A dog mailman.. ______
A surfboard... ______
A rainbow.. ______
A peace sign.. ______
A pig waving.. ______
A turtle granny carrying groceries...................................... ______
The letters "CC"... ______
A treasure chest... ______
A yellow and orange fish with green fins............................. ______
A ship's anchor... ______
A hot cocoa... ______
A chocolate milk... ______

ABOUT THE CREATORS

Kevin Hoban and Jordan Simkovic have been best friends since meeting at Northwestern University. After college they moved to Los Angeles and began performing for children as the characters "Captain & Cat." Check out their website for kids music, videos and more!

captainandcat.com